# THE MAN WHO FREED THE SLAVES

## STORIES OF FAITH AND FAME
*Edited by Cecil Northcott*

FOREST DOCTOR—*Albert Schweitzer*
TRAIL MAKER—*David Livingstone*
WHITE QUEEN—*Mary Slessor*
LADY WITH A LAMP—*Florence Nightingale*
GOLDEN FOOT—*Judson of Burma*
STAR OVER GOBI—*Mildred Cable*
HORSEMAN OF THE KING—*John Wesley*
CONQUEROR OF DARKNESS—*Helen Keller*
WIZARD OF THE GREAT LAKE—*Mackay of Uganda*
ANGEL OF THE PRISONS—*Elizabeth Fry*
THE MONK WHO SHOOK THE WORLD—*Martin Luther*
YOUNG MAN IN A HURRY—*William Carey*
MAKERS OF THE ENGLISH BIBLE—*The Bible in English*
GOD'S MADCAP—*Amy Carmichael*
SEARCHER FOR GOD—*Isobel Kuhn*
ON THE CLOUDS TO CHINA—*Hudson Taylor*
NEVER SAY DIE—*Gladys Aylward*
QUAKER CAVALIER—*William Penn*
SOUTH SEAS SAILOR—*John Williams and His Ships*
CRUSADER FOR CHRIST—*Billy Graham*
KNIGHT OF THE SNOWS—*Wilfred Grenfell*
FIGHTER FOR THE RIGHT—*Trevor Huddleston*
SAINT IN THE SLUMS—*Kagawa of Japan*
MILLIONAIRE FOR GOD—*C. T. Studd*
SAVE THE CHILDREN—*Eglantyne Jebb*
PROPHET OF THE PACIFIC—*John G. Paton*
THE DOCTOR WHO NEVER GAVE UP—*Ida Scudder*
SLAVE SHIP CAPTAIN—*John Newton*
EVER OPEN DOOR—*Dr. Barnardo*
GOD'S ARCTIC ADVENTURER—*William Bompas*

# THE MAN WHO FREED THE SLAVES

*The Story of William Wilberforce*

by
ELSIE M. JOHNSON

LUTTERWORTH PRESS
GUILDFORD AND LONDON

ISBN 0 7188 2096 7

PRINTED IN GREAT BRITAIN
BY EBENEZER BAYLIS AND SON LTD
THE TRINITY PRESS, WORCESTER, AND LONDON

# CONTENTS

|  |  | *Page* |
|---|---|---|
| 1 | A Boy's Ambition | 7 |
| 2 | The Shrimp Becomes a Whale | 14 |
| 3 | Crusader for Christ | 21 |
| 4 | To Set the Captives Free | 29 |
| 5 | Setback | 37 |
| 6 | The Statesman | 45 |
| 7 | A Bold Experiment | 52 |
| 8 | Distinguished Friends | 61 |
| 9 | Wilberforce at Home | 70 |
| 10 | Wilberforce Writes a Book | 77 |
| 11 | Looking Ahead | 84 |
| 12 | Achievement | 92 |

# 1

## A BOY'S AMBITION

SHOUTS of laughter rang through the class-room. On a table stood a small boy, with eyes full of mischief. He was a born mimic, and at that moment he was delighting his friends by pretending he was the headmaster delivering a lecture to the school. His performance was so entertaining it was as good as a play. He finished with a surprise announcement, "Now boys, you all deserve a half-holiday—class dismiss!"

"Hurrah! Hurrah," responded his companions.

School furniture was overturned, and books were thrown about. Suddenly, a boy at the window signalled,

"He's coming, he's coming!"

Quickly young Willie was lifted from the table by a bigger boy. He was too small to jump down unaided. There was a scramble to gather up the books and papers from the floor. With lightning speed the desks were pushed into straight lines. Each scholar resumed his seat, and began writing in his copy-book. Instead of uproar there was now an uneasy silence.

It was not, however, the Head who quietly opened the door and surveyed the situation. It was an under-master, Mr. Isaac Milner, who happened to be quite a favourite with the pupils. He was a big, burly Yorkshireman.

"Attention, please!" he bellowed, as he took his place in front of the class. The boys obeyed, but looked very uncomfortable.

Milner's bark was worse than his bite. It was all over in a few minutes. Some stern warnings, but no punishment this time. They could all breathe freely once more.

Secretly the under-master admired the little lad who could read and recite and speak so well. He always thought of him as the boy with the musical voice. Indeed, Willie was a likeable child, and it was easy for him to make friends. At seven years of age, he was beginning his education at the Grammar School at Hull.

William Wilberforce—for this was the boy's full name—was born on August 24, 1759. His home was a fine Elizabethan mansion in the High Street of Kingston upon Hull. It was a house with a history. King Charles I had stayed there, in 1639.

Willie's father was a rich merchant, and his mother dreamed of her son growing up, and doing well in life. She pictured him being welcomed into the very best social circles.

Mr. Robert Wilberforce had made much of his fortune by successful trading in the Baltic. Willie loved to hear stories of adventure on the high seas, and tales of foreign lands. Hull is a seaport, and ships of all kinds could be seen at the docks. The boy enjoyed watching the vessels being unloaded, and fitted out for further voyages.

"Hey, Willie," called an older youth, on the quay. "See that ship over there! That one will carry black men in chains across the Atlantic. They are captured in Africa and taken to the West Indies."

"Whatever for?" asked Willie, innocently.

"To work on the sugar plantations, you little stupid," replied the youth. "They make them work hard," he added, with gusto. "Lots of 'em die, but they are only slaves. The white managers soon buy more."

As Willie listened, he shuddered. He felt sorry for the poor black men, and wished he could help them.

\*　　\*　　\*

"I don't want to go home, Auntie," stormed the twelve-year-old, with bitterness in his voice.

"I'm sorry, William, but you will have to go," answered his aunt. She spoke as gently and kindly as she possibly could.

"You see, I have this letter from your mamma. She is coming for you herself, and will take you back to Yorkshire. Of course, your uncle and I will miss you very much."

William tried to hide the tears that would persist in coming to his eyes. When his father died in 1768, he was sent to his uncle's lovely home to be cared for. Going to school at Putney was not very interesting. William, however, did enjoy exploring his uncle's big house; he liked the games in the garden. Most of all, he was impressed

9

by the wonderful stories from the Bible, which his aunt told so vividly.

That morning he found it very hard to eat his breakfast. Then, at last, he managed to ask a question which was worrying him. "Auntie, why must I go home? Have I done something wrong?"

"No, dear William, you have been a good boy." Willie was still not satisfied, so he persisted—

"I'm so happy here, Auntie; do please tell me why I must leave."

Reluctantly, his aunt obliged.

"It is really because I follow the people called 'Methodists', and your mamma does not want *you* to become a Methodist," she said.

Occasionally, when they were gathered round the fire, in the evenings, Willie had heard the word mentioned, but he had never felt that he was involved in any way. Now, however, he was full of curiosity, and full of further questions.

"Who are Methodists, Auntie? It's a funny name." His aunt explained: "A Methodist is one who follows the teaching of John Wesley, and George Whitefield. They are preachers who have done a wonderful work for God. In great open-air meetings, thousands have come together to hear about Jesus, and many have turned to the Lord. Their preaching is simple, so that ordinary folk can understand the meaning."

"Why doesn't Mamma like the preachers?" interrupted the boy.

The answer was given clearly. "Your mamma feels that clergymen should preach only in churches or colleges. She thinks they should not mix with rough, uneducated people."

"Is that all?" exclaimed Willie, in surprise.

"No," continued his aunt, "the Methodists like singing, and Mr. Wesley's brother Charles, has written many hymns. These are sung to lively tunes which people enjoy. Church-goers, however, prefer chants, which are solemn and slow. Your mother would consider the new style isn't a proper way to sing in church."

Mrs. William Wilberforce felt she had talked enough. She would finish by reminding her young nephew of his duty.

"Listen, William," she commanded, "your mamma is a very good woman. I am sure she is doing what she believes is best for you. Do remember that you must love and obey her."

Willie's face was the picture of gloom.

"Yes, Auntie," he murmured, half-heartedly.

As the day advanced, Willie regained his usual, cheerful spirit. He began to think of the exciting 200 mile journey from Wimbledon to Hull. How many times would they stop to change the horses? Where would they stay overnight? Would they be held up by highwaymen?

Before bedtime, Willie ventured one more question about the Methodists.

"Auntie, you didn't tell me how those people got their funny name. I would like to know."

For his benefit therefore, his aunt recalled that when John Wesley was at Oxford, he joined other young University men in forming a club. The aim, she said, was to set aside special times for prayer and Bible study. Later the men would go out and put their beliefs into practice. They had a very strict, careful method in everything they did. Other students at the University noticed this, and nicknamed them Method-ists in fun. The name stuck.

Willie was more than a little interested. He wondered what it was the club went out to do. His aunt told him that the members visited the prisoners in gaol, and took them food. They gathered together poor children who had no schooling, and taught them to read.

"When I grow up, I would like to help people," Willie remarked thoughtfully.

*　　*　　*

His friends in Hull were waiting to give William a tremendous welcome when he arrived home. He received many invitations to great suppers. He was entertained on a lavish scale. This pleased his mother. She hoped it would banish all serious thoughts of religion from his mind.

It was arranged that William should go to Pocklington Grammar School for further education. While there he heard more about the sufferings of the African slaves. It made him feel very unhappy, but what could he do? He was just a fourteen-year-old schoolboy.

"People who feel strongly about anything, write letters to the newspapers," a school-fellow told him one morning after lessons. This gave William a bright idea. He was good at composition. He would write a letter about the poor slaves, and send it to the Editor of the *Yorkshire Gazette*.

\* \* \*

At seventeen, Wilberforce was a wealthy, attractive young man. He loved fine clothes, gay company and popularity. On entering St. John's College, Cambridge, he immediately became a general favourite, for he was warm-hearted, lively and generous. But it was not unusual for rich, fee-paying students to idle away their time at University. While William loved pleasure, he set himself limits. So he steered a straight course, and gave more time to study, than many of his companions.

Before he left Cambridge, he had a goal in view. His ambition was to become a Member of Parliament.

In 1780 that ambition became a reality. William Wilberforce was elected Member of Parliament for Hull. It was a great achievement for a young man of twenty-one.

# 2

## THE SHRIMP BECOMES A WHALE

IT WAS four years later, on a cold and windy
day in March. William edged his way through a
tremendous crowd gathered in the Castle Yard
at York. A political meeting was in progress. He
was scarcely known in the city, and the people
gasped as they watched this slight figure of a man
mount the table which served as a platform. Would
he have strength to battle against the wind and
rain, and make himself heard?

"Who is he?" one said to another.

"Never heard of him", was the general reply.
When the stranger's name was publicly announced,
speculation ceased.

As William began to speak, a hush fell upon the
vast audience. He did not shout. His clear, well-
pitched voice reached the utmost limits of the
crowd. Suddenly an interruption occurred.

A messenger, hot and breathless, with his horse
foaming at the mouth, pushed forward and handed
a note to William. It was a letter from the Prime
Minister, in Pitt's own handwriting. Reading it
quickly, then holding it high for all to see, William
made the most of the dramatic occasion.

"Gentlemen, an announcement from Westminster. I am instructed to inform you that

Parliament is dissolved. The King appeals to the nation," he declared.

The young Prime Minister also ordered, "You must take care to keep all our friends together, and tear the enemy to pieces." It fired William with fresh enthusiasm. He spoke for more than an hour, and held his listeners spell-bound. No one wanted to go home. The famous man-of-letters, James Boswell, was in the crowd, and was amazed: "I saw what seemed a mere shrimp mount upon the table, but as I listened he grew and grew, until the shrimp became a whale," he said with admiration.

As William finished speaking, a great shout went up from the Yorkshire freeholders who were present in large numbers. "We'll have this man for our County Member," they proclaimed confidently.

The young politician had won their hearts, and it gave him a sense of thrill and pride. To represent the largest county in England—what an honour! what a prize! Surely it was a mad idea for him to cherish—a dream that would never come true?

That night a big dinner was held at the York Tavern. William was the centre of attraction, and soon the place resounded with cries of "Wilberforce and liberty! Wilberforce and liberty!"

At the General Election, success beyond all expectation came to William. So massive was the support in his favour, and in favour of his colleague, Duncombe, that their rivals acknowledged defeat by show of hands alone, and would not ask for a poll.

"I can never enough congratulate you on such glorious success", read a note from Pitt. Both men indeed had reason to be happy, for the election results as a whole, showed that the nation approved of Pitt's leadership.

William took his seat in the new Parliament on May 14, 1784 as Independent member for the county of York. He celebrated his twenty-fifth birthday and his election victory by having a jolly good time at York Races. He was also planning a holiday abroad. It would be a family party, with his mother and sister and two young ladies who were relatives. He needed another man to join him. Taking an excursion to Scarborough, he was surprised to meet Mr. Isaac Milner, his former tutor—now a Cambridge don. William had a sudden inspiration.

"Mr. Milner!" he exclaimed, "you're the very man I'm looking for. I want you to come with us on holiday." William quickly outlined his plan, and Milner was pleased to accept the invitation. He was nine years older than William, but there was no doubt they would get on well together.

The holiday-makers left for the Continent towards the end of October. On reaching France, they settled at Nice which was a popular resort with the English. Their house overlooked the Mediterranean. Everything seemed to fit in with their carefree spirits—the warm sunshine and the blue sea, the orange groves, and the magic of dining in the open-air. Not least was the pleasure of meeting distinguished people.

A letter from England soon interrupted William's plan. The Prime Minister requested him to return to London urgently for business in Parliament.

Leaving the ladies at Nice, William and his friend set out on the slow homeward journey. Included in their luggage was a book which was to make a very deep impression upon William. It was a book by Philip Doddridge, entitled *The Rise and Progress of Religion in the Soul*. When he had picked it up casually, and asked what the book was about, Milner had replied: "It is one of the best books ever written. Let us take it with us and read it on our journey." It was not an entertaining, enjoyable book, yet it gripped William in a strange, unaccountable way. It caused him to think again of his aunt and uncle at Wimbledon, and the Bible truths they had expounded. For the first time in his life, he felt he was a sinner in God's sight, even though he went to church, and led a most respectable, moral life. It gave him a desire to seek and find God for himself.

As it was winter, the journey across France was full of danger. The snow-bound roads were treacherous. For eighteen days they travelled through blinding snow. In tricky situations, Milner would get out of the carriage, and walk behind and steady it, or he would go forward to guide and encourage the horses.

On the hills of Burgundy death stared them in

the face. As they climbed a frozen road, the weight of the carriage became too much for the horses. They panted and stumbled and showed great fright. Milner realized they were on the edge of a dreadful precipice. He was a man of massive strength. Using all his might, he held on to the carriage and pulled it back, enabling the horses to regain their footing. Thus the fearful plunge to disaster was averted. They were thankful—these two adventurers—when they were back safely in England.

William at once threw himself wholeheartedly into his work. Pitt needed him and he readily responded to the challenge. In his leisure hours, however, the world had a tremendous hold upon him, and the call of God began to fade into the background. He was a member of no less than five famous clubs. Such clubs were popular with politicians, and were very exclusive. They were places where the nation's affairs were discussed, as well as the latest gossip and scandal. Fortunes were squandered at cards—particularly at a game called faro. No one seemed to think of going home until the early hours of the morning.

Being fond of cards, William could have become a victim to the gambling fever. One night his total winnings at the faro table were £600. Immediately afterwards he became unhappy. He realized that the men who had lost their money could ill-afford to do so. They were not wealthy because they had not yet inherited their fortunes. William's sensitive nature was hurt at the thought of doing harm to others. The result was that he soon gave up card-playing altogether.

Another enjoyment which he indulged in was his ability to impersonate prominent people. Since his childhood performance in the classroom at Hull, his power had developed remarkably. At a dinner or supper he would set the whole table laughing uproariously by his perfect imitation of the voice and mannerisms of Lord North. Fortunately someone who had William's best interests at heart was listening and watching. The elderly Lord Camden warned him that mimicry was a dangerous practice for a young politician. William gave heed to the good advice and gave up the habit.

\*       \*       \*

"The Prince says he will come at any time to hear you sing."

This titbit was passed on to William by the Duchess of Devonshire after a soirée at which he first met the Prince of Wales.

With his many accomplishments he was soon inside the magic circle of the great. He was loved by Society for his gaiety and rollicking spirits. Titled ladies were happy when he accepted their invitations. He felt at ease in any company, and he loved to be praised for his singing and dancing.

Would he have to give up all this if he became a Christian?

Sometimes, William asked himself that question

as he crept into bed at four or five o'clock in the morning—after a night of pleasure.

"I will ask Mr. Milner. He is a clergyman and he should know," William told himself, as he went off to sleep.

Soon he would be taking another journey to the Continent and Isaac Milner would go with him. There would be plenty of time then for study and discussion.

# 3

## CRUSADER FOR CHRIST

WILLIAM made his way through the maze of London streets which he knew so well. It was the beginning of December, and he felt the keen, frosty air biting his cheeks and ears with unusual sharpness. He was glad of his heavy cloak. It not only kept out the cold. It concealed the richness of his elegant dress, and partly disguised his identity. He seemed anxious that no one should recognize him, and as he drew near to Lombard Street, he walked more quickly. Another moment, and he had entered the church of St. Mary Woolnoth.

It was Sunday, and a service was about to begin. This church was not his usual place of worship. Rather nervously he walked down the aisle, and slipped into a pew. At last, the gowned figure of the preacher appeared. The sermon was long, but William listened with great attention. The preacher was the minister of the church, the Rev. John Newton, once a slave-ship captain, but now a man of God.

When the service ended, William remained quietly in his pew until almost everyone had left. Then he gathered his cloak around him, picked up his hat, and made his way to the south door.

As he opened it he observed Mr. Newton coming out of his vestry. Here was the opportunity that he had been waiting for.

"Mr. Newton, Sir. May I give you this? It is important."

As he spoke, William drew a letter from the folds of his cloak and placed it in the rector's hands. He felt timid and embarrassed. When he found himself again in the fresh air, he gave a sigh of relief.

John Newton, as soon as he reached home, unfolded the sheet of paper and read it carefully. He was surprised. The writer asked for a meeting with the minister to discuss serious problems. He particularly requested that his visit should be kept secret. The letter was signed, "William Wilberforce."

Newton often received letters of this kind, but he was amazed that so eminent a statesman should seek his help, especially as Wilberforce was looked upon as a man of the world.

Having received the message that the minister was prepared to see him on the Wednesday, William set out early. With time to spare, he walked round and round the Square near Newton's house, thus hoping to gain courage. When he knocked at the door, it was opened by the minister himself, who immediately took William to his study.

"Take a seat, Mr. Wilberforce," he said hospitably, "I shall be interested to hear your story."

"Reverend Sir, I hardly know how to begin," William answered diffidently. "I have had ten thousand doubts, whether or not I should come to you. I am sure it is pride that has kept me back. My friend and tutor, Isaac Milner, suggested that I should seek your advice. He was sure you would be able to help me."

Newton, who had been sitting with head slightly bowed, glanced across at his visitor. William was more relaxed now. His face wore an expression of deep earnestness. There was a compelling urgency in his voice. Newton admired his frankness, and felt his heart warming towards him.

The two men provided a striking contrast. The Rev. John Newton, sixty years of age, wore the dark clothes of a clergyman, but his weather-beaten face and roughened hands told of the hard life of a mariner. Yet there was no hardness in his voice. He spoke gently, causing his hearer to feel instinctively—"Here is a man of sympathy and understanding."

William was dressed in the style of a wealthy young man about town. His large-sleeved loose coat, with its deep lace ruffles and many buttons was immaculately tailored. His long waistcoat had an attractive floral pattern. His wine-coloured velvet breeches were a perfect fit for his slim, shapely legs. He wore silk stockings, and buckled shoes which sparkled and glittered, being held in the gleam of wintry sunshine coming through the study window.

An encouraging word from Newton was the signal for William to proceed.

"There is much to tell you, Sir. I hope I shall not

be tedious. I have but recently returned from the Continent, whither I had gone in order to meet my mother, and bring her and the rest of our party back to England. As on a previous visit, Mr. Milner was with me, and on this latest journey together we derived much profit from our study of the Greek New Testament. It made me feel, Sir, that I wanted to be a Christian in the truest sense of the word."

William paused. "Do go on, Mr. Wilberforce," the minister gently urged.

"Well, early one morning, Mr. Newton, a wonderful thing happened. I was alone, and was reading in St. Luke's Gospel, chapter eleven. Suddenly, some of the verses stood out, as in letters of gold. Maybe you know them. 'Ask, and it shall be given you; seek, and ye shall find ... If ye then, being evil, know how to give good gifts unto your children, how much more shall your heavenly Father give the Holy Spirit to them that ask Him?'

"In a flash, Sir, I knew what I must do. To become a Christian, I needed the Holy Spirit, and I said to myself, 'Let me test this statement. Anyone may do so. I will. God has promised to give His Holy Spirit to those who ask Him. I will go down on my knees and ask.'

"I began to pray earnestly. I was very conscious of my past sins, and condemned myself for having wasted my time and opportunities and talents. But God, for Christ's sake has had mercy upon me. I trust I am a new man inwardly, though as yet there may not be much outward change." William stopped speaking, overcome by emotion.

After a moment's silent prayer for guidance, Newton replied: "It has given me tremendous joy, Mr. Wilberforce, to listen to your testimony. It is, I am sure, only the beginning of what God will do. Greater things are ahead. Now I gather from your letter that you have problems. I would very much like to help you regarding these."

William readily responded.

"My chief problem, Mr. Newton, is this: *'What shall I do with my life?'* Is the Lord saying to me, as to the rich young ruler long ago—'Sell what you have, and give to the poor, and take up the cross, and follow Me.'—?

"Shall I give up politics, and become one of John Wesley's men? Or shall I say goodbye to the attractions of the city, and live a life of prayer and meditation in the quietness of the country?

"Could you advise me, Sir?"

John Newton was a man of discernment. He knew that men of God were needed in public life, and he counselled William: "Do not give up your position in Parliament; do not relinquish your wealth, or forsake your friends. In your chosen career you will find opportunities of advancing the kingdom of God. I advise you, however, to inform the Prime Minister of this change in your life, that he may know where you stand."

William thanked Newton for his advice, and indicated that he would follow it. The two men remained in friendly conversation for a few more minutes. Then in a closing prayer, the minister asked earnestly for God's continued blessing upon the young statesman. As he left the house, William had a wonderful peace in his heart. He knew also he had found a new friend.

*     *     *

At No. 10 Downing Street the Prime Minister was surrounded by piles of official papers requiring his attention. The letter in his hand, however, was not an official document. It was a personal note from Wilberforce, telling of his conversion, and of the new principles which must govern his life. God must be first. William felt he could no longer be a "party man", in politics. There might occur some circumstance in which he could not support Pitt's policies. He told Pitt that he would always have a strong affection for him, and he hoped that their personal relationship would be unchanged.

In reply, Pitt wrote a most generous letter of some 700 words, ending: "Believe me, affectionately and unalterably yours, W. Pitt."

The next day he went to see William, and spent two hours with him. The happy outcome was, that while Pitt could not understand the spiritual experience of which William spoke, the two men remained firm friends.

With his new outlook on life, William became more and more aware of the many bad things in the land. There was much wickedness among the upper classes, as well as among the poor.

In eighteenth-century England the poorer classes

of society had a very hard life. Not only men, but women and young children worked long hours in factories, which were dark, damp and unventilated. The pay was miserably small. Children became permanently bent and deformed because of their work. Whole families lived at starvation level.

Yet if a half-starved man stole a loaf of bread to feed his hungry children, he could be transported; if a peasant stole a sheep he could be hanged.

There was much drunkenness and gambling, cruelty, blasphemy and immorality among rich and poor alike.

William, zealous for God, was anxious to see an improvement in the nation's morals. He succeeded in enlisting support for a society which would fight the evils of the day. The King was approached, and a Royal Proclamation against Vice and Immorality was issued on June 1, 1787.

Setting out from London, William visited the bishops and high-ranking church officials to obtain their co-operation and interest. Likewise, he visited the noblemen in their stately homes. Sometimes he was well received, and sometimes he was rebuffed.

"So you wish to be a reformer of men's morals?" questioned one nobleman, scornfully. Then, pointing to a picture of the Lord dying on the Cross, he added: "Look then, and see there, what is the end of such reformers."

The crusader for Christ listened, but went on his

way undaunted and unafraid. When the Proclamation Society, as it was called, was launched, it did two very good things. It encouraged the stricter observance of Sunday, as God's Day, and it checked the circulation of bad literature.

# 4

## TO SET THE CAPTIVES FREE

HE WAS enjoying a visit to the Premier's country house at Holwood, with its thirty or forty acres of woodland. It seemed to William to be a grand opportunity to speak to Pitt on a subject which was causing him great concern. It was the subject of slavery. The horrible, mental picture of black men in chains, had remained with him through the years. Now, having gathered a great deal of information about the shameful trade, William wanted to raise the matter in Parliament. He found the Prime Minister most sympathetic and helpful. In fact, Pitt felt that William's character and talents eminently fitted him to lead an anti-slavery campaign.

Both men were aware that any move to halt the traffic in Negro slaves would be bitterly opposed. Britain's international trade and economy was completely dependent upon it.

The trading route was England, Africa, the Americas, and return to England. Ships reached Africa laden with iron and copper bars, linen and cotton cloth, woollen materials, knives and spearheads, firearms and spirits, as well as cheap trinkets. These were bartered for black people who had been captured, put in chains and brought to the coast. They were then herded on to the ship, and had to endure a dreadful journey to the West Indies by a route known as the "Middle Passage". The death rate was very high. No wonder, for the Negroes—men, women and children—were packed like sardines on the lower decks and in the hold. Specially constructed narrow shelves were fitted, so that the maximum number of slaves could be stowed in the vessel. The victims had no room to turn; no room to move. Often the men were kept shackled. The women were shamefully abused by the sailors. There was very little ventilation, and no sanitary arrangements. The captives who survived this ordeal were sold to the "planters"— plantation owners or managers.

Ships arrived back in England carrying sugar. It was an expensive luxury loved by the British people, who had no idea of the cost to the black man in unhappiness, physical suffering, and perhaps death, through ill-treatment.

Few voices had been raised in protest. Among the few who had shown concern was the Christian group known as the Society of Friends, or "Quakers". Later, John Wesley and his supporters had followed their lead.

One day in 1765 an incident occurred which had far-reaching results. It happened that a young clerk employed in the Army Ordnance Department was walking in Mincing Lane, London, when he heard cries of pain and terror. A Negro slave had been beaten by his master, and thrown into the street to die. Young Granville Sharp, though

sickened by the sight, was stirred into action.

"My God! I must do something to help that poor fellow," he muttered.

He hurried to the spot, and lifting the black man from the gutter, he took him to the surgery of his brother William. Not only did the Negro receive medical treatment. Granville Sharp, like the Good Samaritan of old, provided the injured man with shelter and money. Having such care and attention, he made a good recovery. When Sharp found work for him at an apothecary's, all went well with the Negro for quite a long time. Then came a dark day for Jonathan Strong, as the Negro was called. Unexpectedly his old master met him in the street. A quick glance was sufficient to convince the wicked man that Jonathan was now fit for hard work.

"I'll get him," he threatened. "That nigger belongs to me. Well fed and fattened, he looks quite a gentleman. A few months back on the plantations will soon alter that."

David Lisle, the planter from Barbados gave a cunning, malicious laugh, and acted quickly. He paid two seamen to kidnap Jonathan, and then proceeded to sell the Negro for £30 to a man returning to Jamaica. Lisle did not know that someone else was also acting swiftly.

The news about Jonathan had reached Granville Sharp just in time. He rushed off to see Sir Robert Kite, the Lord Mayor of London, and Jonathan was set free on the grounds that he had been deprived of his liberty without a warrant. As the parties left the Court, a last desperate bid was made to lay hold of the Negro, and drag him away from his friends. The attempt failed.

This case was not an isolated one, for there were many slaves in England at that time. By the end of the century it was estimated that 14,000 slaves lived here.

It had become fashionable for planters, when they returned to England, to bring some of their domestic slaves with them. These plantation owners were the newly rich of that day. They lived in big houses, and gave lavish parties. They enjoyed showing off, and one way of doing so was to dress a well-trained Negro in resplendent uniform, and use him as a footman, or a carriage flunkey.

Most slaves in England were fairly well treated by their masters, and were contented. There were, however, some exceptions, and unhappy, badly treated slaves would sometimes make a dash for freedom. Even with a dark skin, it was possible to get away, unnoticed, in the London crowds, but it was a risky venture. Masters were not prepared to lose their property so easily. They would hunt down the runaways and bring them back, using force if necessary.

When people in the city streets saw a terrified Negro being dragged by an angry master back to captivity and punishment, their sympathies usually were with the black man.

Granville Sharp pressed forward in his efforts on behalf of the slaves, for while he was happy with the outcome of the Jonathan Strong battle, one victory only, was not sufficient to satisfy him. In 1772, he was given the opportunity he had long been waiting for. A test case concerning a runaway Negro named James Somerset was fought through the courts. After three sittings, Lord Chief Justice Mansfield delivered judgment. There were gasps of dismay from the planters, as he declared: ". . . the claim of slavery never can be supported . . . the black must be discharged."

It was an historic decision; the day on which it was handed down—June 22, 1772—was a day to be remembered. The ruling meant that as soon as any slave set foot on English ground he became free. Slavery in Great Britain was abolished by this judgment, but it did not affect British possessions overseas, where slavery would continue to exist for another sixty years.

Naturally, Sharp was encouraged by Lord Mansfield's verdict, but he felt there still was much more to be done, and he seemed alone in the conflict. He did not know that God was preparing others to join him in a great Anti-Slavery Campaign.

\*     \*     \*

A young man named Thomas Clarkson was determined to win the prize offered by Cambridge University in 1785, for an essay in Latin. The subject was an unusual one—"Is it right to make slaves of others against their will?"

It meant months of hard work, gathering

information. Clarkson devoured all the books he could find on the subject. He sought out military men who had served in the West Indies and knew the facts of the African slave trade. The theme gripped him, and he succeeded in winning the award. Then he found he could not dismiss the matter from his mind. It haunted him night and day. As he wandered in the woods near his home, again and again he said to himself: "Those poor slaves! Those poor slaves! Surely someone must intervene."

Before long the young graduate saw clearly what he himself must do. Riding through Hertfordshire on his way to London, suddenly and dramatically he received what he believed to be a direct call from God. It was a challenge to devote the whole of his life to the destruction of the slave trade. Clarkson dismounted. Holding his horse, he knelt in prayer on the turf by the roadside, and promised obedience to God's call.

He translated and published his prize essay. Soon he was brought into touch with the Quakers, and with Granville Sharp. The little group met often to talk about the subject uppermost in their minds. In the summer of 1787 a Committee for the Abolition of the Slave Trade was formed. Granville Sharp was the first Chairman.

These men quickly came to realize that their battle could only be won through Parliament. A politician was needed. He must be a man of sterling character; a man with influence, and a man with the love of freedom aflame in his soul. He must be able to speak well—persuasively and forcefully. His task would be to introduce and carry a Bill through Parliament for the abolition of a trade which they felt was a disgrace to Britain. Could a Member of Parliament be found, who would measure up to their standard, and who would be willing to undertake such a task?

The members of the Committee decided to approach Wilberforce. They were convinced that he was the man they needed. They were pleased when they found him fully prepared to be their spokesman in the House of Commons. He had already received his commission from the Lord.

"God Almighty has set before me two great objects, the suppression of the slave trade and the reformation of manners," William wrote in his journal on Sunday, October 28, 1787.

Wilberforce and Clarkson became great friends. Working like a Trojan, Clarkson visited the slaving ports. Day after day he could be seen talking to merchants and travellers; to ships' doctors and to seamen. He was always jotting down vital information. Often he was in personal danger.

On a dark night at Liverpool docks, a gang of rough men closed in upon him; one of the gang was a known murderer. The sea looked ugly and the tide was running strong. Clarkson at once sensed their evil intention. With one sudden movement, he lowered his head and charged like a bull. He was six foot tall and heavily built. He aimed his blows left and right with terrific force. His enemies were taken by surprise, and he escaped. The next day he returned and continued his investigations as though nothing had happened.

*     *     *

Things were going well with the Abolition Committee. Public interest was being aroused. Petitions denouncing slavery were being sent to Parliament, and Clarkson was granted two private interviews with the Prime Minister. A Committee of the Privy Council was appointed to make a formal inquiry into Britain's commerce with Africa.

Then the blow fell. William was taken seriously ill.

# 5

## SETBACK

**D**ELICATE from birth, with a constant struggle against ill-health, William now lay at death's door. The eminent physicians who were called in predicted that he could not last a fortnight.

In those days it was the usual practice of doctors to send their most important patients to Bath—to recover or die. The sick man therefore was taken to Bath on doctor's orders.

Before leaving home, though extremely weak, William sent an urgent message to Pitt. Unable to eat or sleep, tossed with fever and tormented by thirst, God's servant was worn to a shadow. He was not afraid to die, but one matter was on his heart and mind. It was the slavery question. As the Prime Minister was ushered to his bedside, William with a great effort roused himself to speak. He begged his friend to undertake the Cause, should his own life not be spared to carry it through.

"Wilber, I will move the Resolution in Parliament. I will do all that you would consider proper to do yourself," Pitt answered affectionately.

That dark hour was lit up by the warm glow of friendship. The Prime Minister knew he would have little support from his own party. He knew the King was being influenced against Abolition. Yet he made his promise without reservations.

William was deeply moved. It was more than he had hoped for. He said afterwards that it made him love Pitt more and more. He was able to leave home with his mind at peace.

The Prime Minister kept his word. He himself superintended the Privy Council Inquiry. Then, on May 9, he moved a Resolution binding Parliament to deal with the matter of the slave trade, in the next session. He paid tribute to Wilberforce, and expressed the hope that his honourable friend would be well enough to attend the House, and himself introduce the question, when Parliament re-assembled. Otherwise, Pitt would undertake the task again.

One day about this time, the Member of Parliament for Oxford University, Sir William Dolben, heard that a slave ship was moored in the Thames. He decided to go and investigate. When he saw the arrangements for packing the slaves between the decks—"like books on shelves", as someone described it—he was horrified. He learned that all the slave ships were grossly overcrowded.

Sir William promptly took action in Parliament. He gave notice of a Bill which would regulate the number of slaves carried, in proportion to the tonnage of the vessel. As it was a humanitarian matter—not concerned with the rights and wrongs of slave trading—the House decided that it could be dealt with at once.

The partisans of the trade were furious. They thought only in terms of lost trade and reduced profits, with other disasters to follow. They put up a great fight. The Bill, however, was given a first, second and third reading. Its opponents had one more chance—the House of Lords. Surely the members of the Upper Chamber would throw out the Bill. Indeed, it was violently attacked in the Lords, and it seemed it would be defeated. Hearing how the debate was going, the Prime Minister then declared that if the Bill was rejected, he would not remain in the same Cabinet with the members who opposed it. In the end, Pitt won. By the narrow majority of two votes, the Bill was carried on June 30, 1788, and received the Royal assent on July 11.

\*     \*     \*

In Bath, a miracle happened. William, whose life had hung on a thread, began to recover. Within a month he was well enough to travel to Cambridge, though he had to take the journey very leisurely. Staying in the Master's Lodge at St. John's College, Cambridge, he was happy and comfortable, and benefited by the regular hours, the quietness, and the renewal of friendships. He very much enjoyed the evenings spent with Isaac Milner.

Thus with health gradually improving, he went on to Westmorland. He loved the Lakes, and having a house at Rayrigg, he spent the summer there. He was not without visitors, for even that long ago, it was popular to do "the tour of the Lakes".

Later, William went to town and dined with Pitt; paid a visit to Yorkshire, and made another journey to Bath—this time, not as an invalid, but as a man with renewed vigour.

Throughout his convalescence, William kept in touch with the Abolition Committee. At the beginning of December he was able to again take his place in Parliament.

Back in full harness, William worked day and night in close co-operation with Clarkson, and others of the Abolition Committee. He wanted to be fully prepared for the great debate. In fact, he overtaxed his strength, and when the day arrived—May 12, 1789—he had to admit that he was sadly unfit for work. In spite of physical weakness, however, he spoke powerfully and brilliantly for three and a half hours. The atmosphere of the House was hushed and tense as finally he proposed the motion for Abolition.

Parliament wavered. Its conscience had been aroused, but it was afraid of change. It was fearful lest the interests of the State should be damaged. It was mindful of planters, and others in the trade whose livelihood would be affected.

To the intense disappointment of the campaigners, delaying tactics were adopted, and the vital decision was postponed. Not until April, 1791, was the vote taken. Then the Wilberforce motion was rejected by 163 votes to 88.

William might well have given way to despair, but being a man of faith and courage, when setbacks came he used them as stepping-stones to greater endeavour. There was fresh, up-to-date evidence to be collected, and it was necessary to keep the public well-informed. All this stirred up the malice of extremists in the pro-slavery camp, and the group of ardent Abolitionists knew what it was to suffer persecution. Again and again, the planters or "West Indians", as popularly they were called, tried to blacken William's character. Fortunately, in his case, they were not very successful.

Supported and encouraged by the prayers and the practical help of his friends, William still went forward. John Wesley, just before he died, wrote to him: "If God be for you, who can be against you? Are all of them together stronger than God? Oh, be not weary of well-doing. Go on in the name of God, and in the power of His might."

William Cowper the poet, wrote the *Negro's Complaint*, and thousands of copies were circulated throughout the country:

> Still in thought as free as ever
> What are England's rights, I ask,
> Me from my delights to sever,
> Me to torture, me to task?
> Fleecy locks and black complexion
> Cannot forfeit Nature's claim;
> Skins may differ, but affection
> Dwells in black and white the same.

> Is there, as you sometimes tell us,
> Is there One Who rules on high;
> Has He bid you buy and sell us,
> Speaking from His throne, the sky?
> Ask Him if your knotted scourges,
> Fetters, blood-extorting screws,
> Are the means which duty urges
> Agents of His will to use?

Josiah Wedgwood, the master-potter, had a cameo made, with the picture of a Negro kneeling, and begging for mercy. Before long it was seen on the lids of gentlemen's snuff-boxes, being inlaid in gold. It was inserted in ladies' bracelets, and other jewellery. Again, some people as a protest against slavery, stopped using West Indian sugar, and thousands continued to sign petitions, which were promptly sent to Westminster.

Early in 1792 another great Parliamentary debate took place. William rose once more to make his proposal for Abolition. Henry Dundas, the Secretary of State for the Home Department, was anxious that things should not move too speedily. When he moved an amendment "That the slave trade ought to be gradually abolished", the amendment was carried by 193 votes to 125.

William was able to see some cause for thankfulness in Parliament's decision. For the first time, a motion for abolition of the slave trade had been carried in the House of Commons, even though it would be abolition by degrees. Others among

William's friends took the view that the amendment was a form of indirect opposition, which
could hinder their Cause for years ahead.

Events in Europe proved to be the main reason,
in point of fact, for halting the progress of the
Wilberforce crusade. The black clouds of the
French Revolution were casting threatening
shadows over England. The Paris massacres in
September, 1792 threw Britain into a state of
shocked alarm. The execution of Louis XVI, a few
months later, gave Englishmen a further nasty jolt.
Could such things ever happen in this land? they
were asking. Then in February, 1793 the French
Republic declared war on England and Holland—
the Dutch facing invasion.

In these circumstances Parliament had little time
or inclination to give consideration to the slavery
question. Indeed, the Government was facing
serious difficulties at home. There was unemploy-
ment and food scarcity. Radical clubs began to
spring up, and the Government feared an uprising
among the people. Harsh measures were used to
suppress even minor disturbances, and this,
instead of crushing the trouble-makers, made them
still more determined and angry.

Happily, Britain was saved from the fate of
revolutionary France. It was largely because John
Wesley had done his work so well. Thousands had
answered his call to repent of their sins, and give
their lives to Jesus. These people became hard-
working, law-abiding citizens with a healthy
respect for authority. It is true, they often suffered

injustice and hard conditions of life. They did not rebel; they endured in the belief that one day—perhaps far in the future—wrong things would be put right. Above all, they believed there were rewards in Heaven for faithful service.

# 6

## THE STATESMAN

WILLIAM was in his element in Parliament. The rustle of order papers was music in his ears. He loved the thrust of debate, and the magic of good oratory. He sensed the hush in the House, when important decisions were taken. He enjoyed the excitement of victory, and bore bravely the discipline of defeat.

As Members—elegant in embroidered silk and velvet—took their seats in the Commons, it was a colourful scene. The wearing of powdered wigs gave an atmosphere of wisdom and dignity.

Candidature for Parliament was open only to the few. By birth and education, and the liberal endowment of natural talent, William was eminently fitted for the rôle. Throughout his long association with politics, there was but one short period when the daily sitting of the House of Commons lost some of its fascination. It was during the war with France. At first, William supported Pitt but as the war dragged on, he began to ask himself, and his evangelical friends, whether it was right for Christians to continue in it. He was particularly concerned when British troops—so much needed in Europe—were sent to the French West Indies; the intention was to add these rich "sugar islands", as they were called, to the British Empire.

William privately made known his views to the Prime Minister. Then on the floor of the House, he declared that if just and reasonable terms could be negotiated with the enemy, it was advisable and expedient to restore the blessings of peace.

The speech created an explosive situation. There was shock and dismay. The Government was angry, and for the time being the close, strong friendship with Pitt was broken. William felt it keenly. How could he now enjoy attendance at the House? Pitt was there, cold and distant. Former colleagues turned against him, and there were those who sarcastically referred to him as "Citizen Wilberforce".

Happily, this state of affairs did not last long. The rift between the two friends was healed. Both men had been lonely and miserable. Both were glad when once more they could find strength and satisfaction in each other's company.

\*　　\*　　\*

When he entered Parliament, young and attractive, with charming manners and eloquent voice, William immediately became the "darling" of the House. As the years passed, he gained experience. Then his mature judgment and wisdom, linked with his unblemished character, caused men to regard him as an elder statesman, to whom they could look for guidance. Many expected that William would be given high office, or be raised to the peerage. After his conversion however, he ceased to be ambitious for promotion. In later years he expressed his thankfulness that he had been spared these "trappings of greatness".

For thirty years William represented the county of York in Parliament. A General Election was always a significant and notable event. The Election of 1807 proved to be exceptionally exciting. The county was entitled to return two members, and the poll was kept open for fifteen days. The contestants were: Henry Lascelles (Tory), Lord Milton (Whig), Wilberforce (Independent). Each candidate was responsible for his own election expenses. Milton and Lascelles were each prepared to spend £100,000 on the election, and had made up their minds that at all costs they must secure the two seats. While these two had behind them the resources of their respective political parties, William, being an Independent, had no party to support him. He certainly was a man of means, but he had not the long purse of his opponents.

On nomination day a member of William's audience made a generous gesture.

"We cannot desert Mr. Wilberforce," he said. "I put down my name for £500." Others followed his example, and about £18,000 was immediately subscribed. Soon, money was flowing in from every part of the country until a total of £70,000 was reached. William did not use the whole amount. More than half was returned to subscribers.

Finance was not the only obstacle to overcome. William discovered that Milton and Lascelles had got in first and hired every available vehicle to take voters to the poll. There was not a gig or carriage or military car to be had. Resourceful and resolute Yorkshiremen, in support of Wilberforce, found other means of transport. Farmers lent their wagons; some folk rode on donkeys, while hundreds went on foot. Boats, large and small, proceeded up-river carrying their passengers to the poll. For fifteen days and nights both work and sleep were forgotten. Perhaps a tired messenger might be seen dozing upon his posthorse, or in his carriage. Voters came from the remotest corners of the county, so every day the roads were crowded. Market squares and city streets were filled with people curious to hear the latest news.

William's election meetings were broken up frequently by toughs and bullies. He found it most difficult to get a hearing. On the twelfth day he felt ill, and had to keep to his room. Then the rumour was circulated, "Wilberforce is dead." The lie was soon killed. His opponents had done their worst, but it availed them nothing. William's victory was secure. At the final count, the figures read:

> Wilberforce, 11,806
> Milton, 11,177
> Lascelles, 10,989

Just prior to this election victory—before the dissolution of Parliament—William had experienced the most triumphant moment of his life. The date was February 23, 1807. Before Parliament was a "Bill for the Abolition of the Slave Trade".

The fierce opposition of former years had vanished. Few were prepared to speak against the Bill. There was mounting excitement in the House. Speaker after speaker waxed eloquent in favour of Abolition, and praised the Private Member who had battled for more than twenty years on behalf of the Negroes. At last Romilly, the Solicitor-General, rose and wound-up for the Government. Confident that Wilberforce would win, he spoke of "the innumerable voices that would be raised in every quarter of the world to bless him . . . having preserved so many of his fellow-creatures".

The House was on its feet immediately. The cheering of three hundred M.P.s resounded through the Chamber. William was given an ovation such as the House had given to no other living man. Overwhelmed with emotion, he sat in his seat with his head in his hands. The tears were streaming down his face.

The excitement increased when it was announced that 283 had voted in favour of the Bill. Only sixteen were against. Later, a few close friends gathered in William's house. They were jubilant.

"Well, Henry, what shall we abolish next?" William inquired light-heartedly. He was addressing the question to his cousin Henry Thornton, who was also an M.P. A little later William was asked a question. He was kneeling on one knee at a crowded table, busy scribbling a note, when someone piped up, "What are you writing? Put down the names of those sixteen miscreants who voted against us."

Looking up quickly, William answered: "Never mind the miserable sixteen. Let us think of our glorious two hundred and eighty-three."

The gathering broke up. The friends left, and William was alone. He felt it was not the time for self-satisfaction and boasting. Instead, he was filled with humility and thankfulness to God. Then his thoughts turned to the nation. "God will bless this country," he whispered to himself.

William allowed his thoughts to run on and on. He remembered the work done by the Abolition Committee. How diligently each member had worked.

There was John Newton too. He could never forget dear old John who had given him such encouragement at the beginning of his Christian life, and had remained his friend through the years. What a help it had been to the Anti-Slavery crusade when Newton had published in 1788 a record of his own personal experiences.

John Newton had lived in a crowded slave-ship. He had been captain of a desperate crew. His account of the ghastly facts had stirred many hearts, and caused many people to change their opinions about the slave trade.

"I must go myself, and tell dear John the good news," William decided. "How his face will light up, when he hears."

On March 25, the King assented to the Bill, and it became law. The Act provided that after May 1, 1807 the African slave trade, "and all manner of dealing and trading" in the purchase of slaves in

Africa, and in their transport from Africa to the West Indies, or to any other territory, was "Abolished, prohibited, and declared to be unlawful".

The Abolitionists could well pause in their endeavours, and rejoice in this significant advance. Their final goal, however, was the abolition of slavery itself, with international agreement. There was still much ground to be covered.

It might have been supposed that William was giving so much of his time to the anti-slavery movement, that some parliamentary duties would be neglected. This was not the case.

He was regular in his attendance at the House. He gave careful attention to the great questions of the day. He served on parliamentary committees. He looked after the interests of his constituents. If they desired to have a word with their M.P., he was ready to receive them and deal with their problems. When they wrote to him they were sure of having a prompt reply.

# 7

## A BOLD EXPERIMENT

A NEW and exciting experiment was suggested to William and his friends. It made a strong appeal, for it was designed to help the Negroes.

The idea was to establish a colony in Africa where black men could work in favourable conditions, at farming and simple crafts. A certain explorer named Dr. Henry Smeathmam, had recommended Sierra Leone on the west coast of Africa, as being suitable for the project.

The first settlers would be emancipated slaves from England—principally Negroes who had refused to work for their old masters, when slavery became illegal in this country. In the course of time, these black men had found their way to the big cities. An ever-increasing number were roaming the streets of London. They were out-of-work, unwanted and hungry, and were obliged to beg for food.

Granville Sharp and his colleagues did much for the relief of the sufferers, but there was a limit to their resources. The British Government, also, was aware of the situation, and regarded it with growing concern. It came to be known as the problem of "the black poor".

The Sierra Leone scheme appeared to offer a

solution. It would give these Negroes a new start in life, and from the Government point of view, would rid the country of unwanted men. The Negroes would be transported in one group from London to their native Africa.

With State support, therefore, the Abolitionists were encouraged to go forward. Plans were finalized, and a ship sailed with 340 Negroes, and a few skilled white craftsmen. The Abolitionists, however, were very displeased when they discovered that the Government had arranged to transport in the same vessel, other unwanted people—some white women of low moral character.

"It will give a wrong impression! It will not be good for the Negroes," said William and his friends.

At last the ship reached its destination, Sierra Leone, the place that had been pictured as a haven of happiness and security for the black men.

Alas! the venture was not a success. Disease and death overtook some, for the climate was unhealthy, even for people who had been born in that country. Others deserted, and ran away into the interior.

Joshua and Samuel were two who, a few months after arrival, decided to make their escape.

\*    \*    \*

"Wake up, Samuel," whispered Joshua to the young boy who lay beside him. "It's time to be moving," he urged.

Samuel was not really asleep. He had been waiting for this word from his friend. Now, when he heard his name and felt a gentle nudge, he answered at once.

"Yes, Joshua, I'm ready." He had to speak very quietly, for there were others in the hut, and he must not disturb them.

Joshua was about nineteen years old, and Samuel was fourteen. They still called each other by the English names given to them by the planters. Though they liked the Governor of the colony, and were pleased to have regular meals, and work that was not too hard, they longed to be completely free. Joshua remembered his own tribal village. If only they could find the way back, and meet their own people again! They did not understand the vastness of Africa, and the dangers they would encounter.

Leading the way to the end of the building, Joshua stepped very softly. The hut was only a temporary shelter, used to house some of the Negroes in the good weather. A weak place in the wall served Joshua's purpose. With little effort, and no noise, he made a hole large enough to crawl through. Safely on the outside, the runaways paused for breath, but they knew they must not linger.

At first they crept stealthily in the shadows of the settlement buildings. As soon as they were clear of the compound, they ran towards the woods. The coast road would have been easier, but they had heard that slave-traders still operated in the area. These bad men were ever on the look-out for fugitives from the settlement. Reaching the foot of the mountains, Joshua and Samuel began to climb. It was hard going, but they pressed on hour after hour, until the heat became unbearable.

They were glad to stop after a while, and rest in the shade of the forest trees which clothed the lower slopes. Joshua had smuggled flasks of water, and a good supply of cooked rice from the colony, together with a cook's knife which he had found lying on the kitchen table. As they ate and drank, he told Samuel of the animals that lived in the forest—the chimpanzees, the tiger-cats and the bush pigs. He said he would set snares for small animals, and they could skin and eat them. He wished he had fire-arms like the white men used.

"Shall we fish in the rivers?" asked Samuel.

"Yes, we shall be able to get plenty of fish," said Joshua. "I expect we shall see hippos, and crocodiles too," he added.

Before darkness fell, the two climbed to a vantage point, to spy out the land. Far in the distance they could discern a ribbon of mountain-trail, descending to some unknown village. Looking backward, from whence they had fled, they could dimly make out the contour of the settlement buildings on the coastland.

During that night, Joshua slept fitfully, and then wakened with a sense of fear and dread. Stepping out from the leafy shelter he had made for Samuel and himself, he gave a cry of horror.

"Samuel, come here, and look what's happening," he called urgently. His young companion was at his side in a moment. "Look, Samuel, across there! It's miles away, but that's our colony on fire."

Joshua's words were all too true. The settlement was ablaze. What was the cause?

A few days earlier, the settlement people had met with hostility from a neighbouring tribe which was suspected of carrying on the slavery business. British sailors had then raided and destroyed the tribal village. In revenge, the local chief, who had escaped injury, marched into the settlement, intent on burning it to the ground.

Joshua and Samuel had tears in their eyes as they watched the red glow on the horizon. They spoke in subdued tones. They wondered how many of their friends had died, and how many were safe.

*     *     *

Time passed. Joshua reached full manhood, and was tall and strong. Samuel developed too, and became an expert hunter. In the dry season they lived in the forests, but would make their way to the villages, before the rains came. They were good workers, and could always find employment. One thing caused them sorrow. They had never been able to find their own tribe and people.

Occasionally, through the grape-vine, they heard news of the colony. It seemed the pioneers would never give up. Every time the place was raided, and looted and set on fire, it was rebuilt on a grander scale. They were told of a new capital,

called Freetown, with church and hospital, schools
and warehouses.

★     ★     ★

"It is time we were setting off for the forests,
Samuel. The rains have ceased. Tomorrow we shall
start our journey," announced Joshua, one fine
morning. Samuel was pleased. For weeks past,
they had been living in a friendly village. A kind-
hearted woodman and his wife had given them
lodging. The peasant couple had an only son, who
was called Danie. He was about ten years old, and
Samuel and he had become great friends.

That morning, Danie had gone with his father
and other villagers to cut wood. During the tree-
felling operations, a dreadful accident occurred.
Danie heard a warning shout, but it was too late.
A falling tree pinned him to the ground, by his
foot. He gave a cry of pain, and became uncon-
scious. His father ran to him, and with the other
men using all their strength, they slowly released
the boy from the heavy weight. His foot was
terribly crushed.

"He will die! He will die! My only son will die,"
cried his father. "I should not have let him come.
He should have stayed with his mother."

Slowly they carried Danie home, and laid him
on his own little bed. He had regained conscious-
ness, but was in great pain, and delirious with fever.

"What shall we do? What shall we do?"
moaned his parents, again and again, as they
watched him.

57

Samuel crept in to see poor Danie, and then turned his head, and cried. Later, he spoke up: "Take Danie to white man. Take poor Danie to white man," he implored. "White man's medicine will take away fever; white man will heal poor Danie's foot."

The boy's father answered sharply: "White man is bad man; white man kills black man."

At that moment Joshua came in, and spoke of the white doctor's skill and kindness.

After much persuasive talk, Danie's father at last agreed to take Danie to the white doctor in Freetown. It was a last hope—the only hope of saving his life.

Samuel offered to set out at once for the settlement. He would act as runner, and arrive first at the hospital, to give information about Danie's condition. The seriousness of the case called for quick decisions. Samuel's offer was accepted. It was then arranged that at first light Danie's father and Joshua would follow, carrying the injured boy on a litter, or stretcher. Two trusted men from the village would go with them, to carry provisions.

Samuel started off immediately. He knew the forests and the mountain paths well, and ran on and on, through the delicious coolness of the night. He covered the miles with remarkable speed. Sometimes, he was up to his waist in mud. Sometimes, he was drenched and almost drowned, as he forded swollen rivers. There were occasions when huge boulders blocked his way. It mattered not to Samuel. He was determined to get to Freetown.

He saw the dawn breaking; he saw the sun start its journey, but not until it reached its meridian did he rest. All he needed was a scanty meal, and to snatch a few hours' sleep. Then, on and on he went, continuing through that night also.

The next morning, Samuel got a glimpse of Freetown on the skyline. He was tired by this time, but he still had a long way to go. It was nightfall when he reached the settlement, and knocked for admittance. Before the door could be opened, he had sunk to the ground, weak and utterly exhausted, and unable to speak. Kind hands lifted him, and brought him inside. He was washed, and his nasty scratches and bruises were gently rubbed with soothing, healing ointment. They gave him a nice white shirt, and a good meal. After that, he felt better, and was able to tell them about Danie.

*   *   *

High up in the hills, in a spot shaded by trees, the hospital party came upon poor Danie, very weak and ill. His father felt sure he could not live much longer. Joshua was there, and the two porters, all looking very sad.

The white doctor carefully examined the little boy. He gave him medicine to stop the raging fever, but as he looked at the mutilated foot, his face grew more serious. He took Danie's father aside, and spoke to him in a grave voice, using Joshua as interpreter. An immediate operation was essential. Every moment was precious. The injured foot was already turning septic, and must be amputated.

Danie's father hesitated.

"Say yes," urged Joshua, pleadingly.

"Yes, Doctor, you can do it," the father bravely answered.

The doctor bowed his head in prayer. His assistants opened a folding table, which they secured firmly to the ground. Danie was gently lifted, and prepared for the operation. An armed escort, which had accompanied the hospital workers, stood guard.

"It is well with your son." The doctor spoke reassuringly to Danie's father, when it was all over. The sick boy was taken to Freetown to be cared for, until he was well again, and his leg was healed. Then there was great rejoicing.

\*    \*    \*

Joshua and Samuel had been doing some hard thinking. They decided to give up their forest wanderings, and to go back to the settlement to live. Samuel had been told that the colony would welcome them.

It made them very happy when they were allocated their own piece of land to cultivate, and were supplied with seed, and good farming implements.

Mr. Zachary Macaulay, the new white Governor, was a kind, good man who was greatly admired by the Negroes. It was said that he had been specially chosen for the post, by Mr. William Wilberforce, the black man's friend in London.

# 8

## DISTINGUISHED FRIENDS

IN THE meantime, William was becoming more and more powerful in Parliament, while in social circles his charming personality continued to delight his friends, and dismay his critics. The Prime Minister, William Pitt, always held a special place in his affections, in spite of the strain of the war years.

It was a life-long friendship, for the two had known each other at Cambridge. However, it was in London, in the Gallery of the House of Commons, in 1780, when they were really drawn together. Both were interested in political debate, and both wanted to climb the ladder to parliamentary success. Thus, with common interests, they would spend their nights together at the famous Goosetree's Club. At week-ends, Wilberforce would invite Pitt to his villa at Wimbledon. There, business cares would be forgotten, and they would be as happy as schoolboys on holiday.

They would go fishing, or riding, or walking. In the dusk, they would chase one another round the garden, then dine together, or with specially invited guests. William admired Pitt's ready wit; and they vied with each other in the art of repartee, "foyning", or "foining", it was called in those days.

Pitt wanted to improve his French, so a grand tour of France was arranged for the autumn of 1783. The two friends, with a Mr. Eliot (who afterwards became Pitt's brother-in-law) journeyed via Dover and Calais. At the town of Rheims, the arrival of three strange Englishmen caused great concern to the Superintendent of Police.

"They have no servants; they have settled in poor lodgings, yet one of them pretends to be the son of the great Earl of Chatham," he told the Abbé de Lageard, who was a high official of the town.

"Do nothing in a hurry. I will see them myself, and report back to you," replied the Abbé.

Once the genuineness of the Englishmen's claims was established, the principal families in Rheims hastened to invite Pitt and his companions to their homes. Often there were amusing episodes. Invited one evening to the house of a wealthy wine-merchant, they surveyed with pleasure the rich delicacies set before them. They were puzzled, however, by a large vacant space right in the centre of the table. Still more intriguing were the smiles and whispers of the assembled guests.

Soon the mystery was solved. A door opened, and two servants entered carrying between them a huge dish of roast beef. This was put down with some ceremony, in the middle of the table, in the place reserved for it. The joint was carved, and the Englishmen were invited to enjoy the feast. The beef was almost raw, and not one of the three could touch it.

The French were very disappointed, but fortunately not offended. They came to the conclusion that the visitors were unwilling to display their national tastes before strangers.

Moving on to Paris, and to Fontainebleau, the tourists found no lack of excitement. Introduced at Court, they were dazzled by the beauty and the engaging manner of Queen Marie Antoinette. In contrast, Louis XVI was seen as a strange, clumsy figure. In his immense boots, "it was worth going a hundred miles for a sight of him, a-boar-hunting," Wilberforce declared.

The holiday came to an abrupt end. A special messenger from London brought a summons to Pitt to return immediately. The Coalition Government was about to fall. The friends arrived home to find London agog with rumours. Soon, Pitt himself was in the place of power, for in December, 1783, he became Prime Minister.

At the age of twenty-four, William Pitt attracted attention as the youngest Prime Minister in English history. In public life, he was regarded as the cold, haughty statesman—almost unapproachable, but he was a man of integrity, hating bribery and corruption. He loved his country with passionate devotion. Indeed, almost his last words when he died, were, "Oh! my country! How I love my country!" Pitt died at the early age of forty-seven. His interest in the abolition of the African slave trade was genuine, though at times variable. In one great speech, we find him looking far into the future, and catching the vision of Africa civilized, with slavery abolished, and the natives engaged in industry and commerce—enjoying, indeed, the blessings which Britain enjoyed.

Wilberforce felt the loss of his friend keenly. His deepest sorrow was that during all the years of close acquaintance, he had not been able to bring Pitt over to the Lord's side.

\*    \*    \*

When William met Hannah More, he was immediately drawn to her, for he at once perceived that her spirit was akin to his own. The feeling was mutual, for in a letter written from Bath in the autumn of 1787, Hannah declared: "I find here a great many friends. Those with whom I have chiefly passed my time are Mr. Wilberforce's family. That young gentleman's character is one of the most extraordinary I ever knew, for talents, virtue and piety. It is difficult not to grow wiser and better, every time one converses with him."

Hannah was a vivid, arresting personality, who as a writer and dramatist, had gained a high literary reputation. She frequently visited London, where she enjoyed the patronage and friendship of the great. David Garrick, the renowned English actor, welcomed her. The distinguished portrait painter Sir Joshua Reynolds, took an interest in her, and Dr. Samuel Johnson, of dictionary fame, made much of her.

There came the time, however, when Hannah More grew rather weary of the attractions of the world. The impact of the spiritual movement, known as the Evangelical Revival, was reaching the upper crust of Society, and Hannah was influenced by it. She went to hear John Newton preach; she drew closer to those people whom, she felt, had a definite Christian experience. Before long, she too, gave her heart to Christ, and decided to use her talents in His service. It was at this period that William was brought in touch with her. They became life-long friends.

There were occasions when Hannah loved to get away into the country. Cowslip Green was the name of her one-storey thatched cottage at Wrington, in Somerset. From her drawing-room windows, she had a splendid view across the valley to the Mendip Hills. The Downs stretched for miles like extensive lawns, kept neat and trim by the grazing of the sheep. There were places where wild flowers grew in profusion, and watercress could be gathered from the running streams.

The Cowslip Green garden was Hannah's pride. So much of her time and attention was given to it, that sometimes she felt a little guilty, afraid that it might become an idol in her heart. Still, it gave much pleasure to her many visitors, and Hannah was one who was good at entertaining her friends.

William found that a visit to Cowslip Green always acted like a tonic. It was not only the country air, the quietness, and the beautiful scenery; what he appreciated most was the opportunity of talking about the deeper things of God, to one who fully understood.

In the autumn of 1789, William and his sister were staying at the cottage, and were urged to take an excursion to the famous Cheddar cliffs. The grandeur of the place impressed them both, but the spiritual condition of the people, and their poverty, greatly distressed William. Such ignorance, and such lack of comfort simply appalled the good man. He was so upset by what he saw, that his appetite left him, and he could not eat the refreshments which had been packed and placed in his carriage. As soon as he got back to the cottage, he went straight to his room, and remained alone. His sister thought he must be ill, yet at supper-time, when he reappeared, he seemed entirely different—as though he had been sustained by heavenly food.

When the servant had left the room, William began to speak in earnest, compelling tones: "Miss Hannah More, something must be done for Cheddar."

Hannah, and her young sister Martha (affectionately known as Patty), listened and discussed plans until the hour was late.

"If you will be at the trouble, I will be at the expense," William promised.

It did not take long for Hannah to come to an agreement. Later, Patty gave her own reaction: "Something seemed to tell me it was the Lord's work," she said.

The plan was to start Sunday Schools in the villages, as Robert Raikes had done in Gloucester in 1780.

Very soon, Henry Thornton became deeply interested, and joined William in financing the work. Henry was not only a Member of Parliament; he was also a rich and influential banker. He had a magnificent home on Clapham Common. It was a spacious Queen Anne house with thirty-four bedrooms. A fine oval library—designed by William Pitt—was added to the original building.

Henry Thornton called his house Battersea Rise, and he shared it with William for about four years. This was a happy arrangement, for Wilberforce was his friend and kinsman.

Clapham in those days was completely rural. The villas and mansions of wealthy men ringed the common. Quite a number of these men were keen, evangelical Christians, so at Clapham, William was, indeed, among his friends. They met in each other's homes to talk, and to pray. They went to church together, taking their families with them. Afterwards, they discussed the Sunday sermon.

The group felt privileged in having the Rev. John Venn as Rector of Holy Trinity, Clapham—where they worshipped. Such was their interest in his preaching, they would write out extracts from his sermons, and send to friends who had been absent from church. William appreciated those sermons, for he always enjoyed a good spiritual meal.

On one occasion he reported: "How excellent a sermon has Venn been preaching upon Luke chapter 14:28—counting the cost if we profess to be Christians. It affected my heart, it humbled me in the dust. My days pass away in hurry . . . Oh, may I wait on God diligently."

John Venn supported the group in their crusade for the Abolition of Slavery. He was an esteemed member of this circle of friends, whom some people began to call the "Clapham Sect". Others named them "the Saints", and the term was not always used in derision. Nevertheless, they were not stained glass window saints with halos.

Their religion did not make them stiff and starchy, or solitary and gloomy. They enjoyed life to the full. They lived according to their station in life, with homes richly furnished and tables well spread. They had their domestic servants, their carriages and their coachmen. They loved company, especially each other's company. Friends and relatives of one member of the group were always welcome in the homes of the others. Those like Hannah More who visited from a distance, were given hospitality in lavish manner.

Battersea Rise was the venue for the most important gatherings of the Clapham team, the famous library being ideal for the purpose. Indeed, it became the crusaders' headquarters.

Wilberforce was the undoubted leader of the band, and Henry Thornton was next in prominence. Granville Sharp was the oldest member in point of age, and Zachary Macaulay the youngest. Indeed, Macaulay was only twenty-six, when he was appointed Governor of Sierra Leone. Among the "Saints" he was noted for his extraordinary memory. If a date or fact or quotation needed verification, there was no need to consult an encyclopaedia.

"Look it up in Macaulay," they said.

In the group there were others who had distinguished themselves in the service of the nation. Truly, the Clapham Sect comprised a company of remarkable men, and William was proud to count them his special friends.

# 9

## WILBERFORCE AT HOME

VERY happy in his work, and busy every day, the idea of marriage seemed far removed from William's thoughts. Then the unexpected happened. While on a visit to Bath, he suddenly fell in love with Barbara Ann Spooner, the eldest daughter of Isaac Spooner of Elmdon Hall in Warwickshire. After a short engagement, they were married on May 30 1797.

"I believe her to be a real Christian, affectionate, sensible, rational in habits, and moderate in desires and pursuits . . ." William declared. The words seem matter-of-fact, but there was no doubt he loved her dearly. John Newton sent congratulations, and another well-wisher, Henry Duncombe, stated: "You will perhaps judge my way of thinking old-fashioned and queer, but I am greatly pleased that you have not chosen your partner from among the titled fair ones of the land . . ."

Barbara's father was, in fact, a Birmingham banker, or merchant.

William took his bride to Cowslip Green for the honeymoon. Hannah More was delighted, giving them a warm welcome, and showering upon them endless kindnesses. Barbara wanted to hear from Hannah's own lips, the story of the Sunday

Schools. For William that story could never be repeated too often.

Thus in the evenings when it was getting dusk, and the lamp was lit and the curtains drawn, the bridal couple would sit and listen as Hannah related what had been done. She and Patty had put forth every effort to reach the children of the farm-hands, the colliers and the glassworkers. When the two sisters started the work, they met with opposition. The clergy were not pleased, the land-owners were against it, and the workers themselves showed no real interest. Threats were made to pull down any schools that were built.

Long journeys were made on horseback over almost impassable roads in order to visit country squires, rich farmers and employers of labour, whose support was necessary if the enterprise was to be a success. The sisters needed great tact as they endeavoured to dispel the nagging fear of the upper classes. These people thought that if the poor were given book-learning, it would make them discontented with their lot, and lead to rebellion. Hannah and Patty assured them that on the contrary, true religion and education for the poor, would mean better work-people, with less poaching and stealing, and damage to property.

It was a long struggle before resistance was broken down, but in the end the ladies won the battle.

Next there was the canvassing of the labourers' families. This was done methodically, but was not easy. Poverty-stricken mothers could not believe that the ladies really wanted to help their children. Surely, there was a catch in it, somewhere.

Hannah and Patty did not give up. Sufficient progress was made to officially open Cheddar Sunday School on October 25, 1789. The building was a place which originally had been used to house oxen. A new roof, flooring and windows gave it a completely transformed appearance. Little was needed at the beginning, in the way of school furniture and equipment. A dwelling was acquired, and converted into a schoolhouse. With a mistress appointed, and scholars recruited, the school had a good start, and became a great success. The main text-book was the Bible.

Inspired by the encouraging results at Cheddar, schools were started in the surrounding villages, and the sisters were full of plans for the future.

The story went on and on, and William and Barbara were always ready for the next instalment. On the Sunday, they visited the schools at Shipham, Axbridge and Cheddar, and were delighted with the progress of the work.

The holiday at Cowslip Green lasted but a few days, and William took his bride to their new home, Broomfield, which was next door to Battersea Rise.

\*     \*     \*

There was plenty of fun and laughter in the Wilberforce household.

William and Barbara were very fond of children. In the course of time, they had four sons and two daughters. As the children grew up, there was no lack of entertainment. They could look forward to parties, with charades, and plays written by Hannah More, lantern shows, and a sumptuous meal as the climax.

In the summer, there were picnics in the country, and excursions to places of interest in the city. There were holidays in the Lake District, and journeys to seaside resorts. Eastbourne, Brighton, Weymouth and Lowestoft were well known to the Wilberforce family.

Friends and acquaintances had nicknames for the boys—Wily Willie and Reliable Robert, Soppy Sam and Hasty Henry.

The parents never tried to crush the high spirits of their offspring. Even when father was in his study downstairs, interviewing an important visitor, and the brothers and sisters were having a noisy game in a room above, there was no sharp word of reproof.

Sunday was a special day, different of course, from the weekdays, but the restrictions were not irksome. To the statesman saint, the Christian faith was such a living, bright reality, that his children caught the joyfulness of it.

In Christian homes in those days it was customary to have family prayers, morning and evening, conducted by the head of the house. At Broomfield, it was most interesting to see the family gather in the dining-room, just before ten o'clock each evening. They were joined by the servants—both men and women domestics—who filed in from the servants' quarters. When the company was complete, each knelt by a chair or sofa. Then Wilberforce knelt at a table in the middle of the room. After a moment of silence, he read three prayers in a low, solemn voice. These devotions took about ten minutes, and were concluded by the repeating of the Grace.

Next, supper was served from a long table drawn up to a sofa where Mrs. Wilberforce was sitting. She presided over the repast, with the help of a Miss Hewitt. The refreshments were ample, including generous slices of cold meat, and various pastries.

William was noted for his kindness to his servants. He was happy with them, and it gave him pleasure to help them. An ex-secretary and an old butler, and others who had given good service, were not dismissed when they became elderly and infirm, but were fitted in to the Wilberforce household. This was much to the amusement of William's friends.

The man who could not bear to cast off an old servant, was also the man who could not tolerate cruelty to animals. One day William was walking up a steep, narrow street in Bath. A horse drawing a cart with a heavy load of coal, stumbled and fell. The coalman was angry, and began to flog the horse viciously. With no thought for his own safety, William quickly stepped forward to intervene. The carter then turned on him with a torrent of abuse, and raised his arm to strike William a violent blow. Fortunately, the coalman's mate stopped the infuriated man: "It's Mr. Wilberforce! It's Mr. Wilberforce! You mustn't hurt him," he cried.

As if by magic, the man's arm dropped to his side, and his face softened: "I'm sorry, sir," he muttered, and helping up his horse, he proceeded on his rounds.

Even the name of Wilberforce had an influence for good, and certainly his advice and help was much sought after, by people in need. In his rooms at Palace Yard, near Westminster, and at his house at Broomfield, he was always available for consultation.

"Mr. Wilberforce, I've run away from home," confessed one young woman, immediately she was admitted into his presence. He dealt with each caller according to the individual need. Always he was courteous and sympathetic, understanding, but firm.

Tramps came, hoping to receive money to help them on their way. Poor clergymen sought his assistance. Statesmen and foreign diplomats waited upon him, to pay their respects. Tribal chiefs, decked in princely regalia, or emancipated slaves in rags—they were all welcomed. It pleased William most of all when Zachary Macaulay arrived with a troop of little black boys from Sierra Leone.

If William was asked how it was he managed to fit so much into each day, he had a simple explanation. He put God first in his life—that was the secret.

He set aside regular times for prayer and Bible reading, and would get up at seven o'clock to spend the first hour of the day alone with his Lord.

"In the calmness of the morning, before the mind is heated and wearied by the turmoil of the day, you have a season of unusual importance for communion with God and with yourself," he said.

Speaking again of his own personal experience, he commented: "I do my work best, when I have most properly observed my private devotions."

# 10

## WILBERFORCE WRITES A BOOK

THERE seemed to be no limit to William's activities, but when he decided to write a book, some of his friends felt it was time to intervene.

His position as a politician was unchallenged. His powers of oratory were outstanding, but his friends had not much confidence that he would shine as a writer. Of course, they always were pleased to receive his letters, but those epistles lacked the magic of his spoken words. It would have been feasible if he had planned to write on parliamentary matters, but for a layman to write a book on religion—and this was William's intention —appeared to them to be illogical. Surely that was the task of clergymen and theologians. Isaac Milner, who by this time had been appointed Dean of Carlisle, did his best to dissuade William. Others also, made known their fears.

The would-be author listened and took note, but he was not deterred from his purpose.

"I laid the first timbers of my tract," he recorded in his diary on August 3, 1793. Thus he pictured his writing as a building, of which he was then laying the foundations. The tract grew into a substantial volume, and was completed in 1797.

"The demand for this kind of literature is very

small," said Mr. Thomas Cadell, the publisher, as William presented his manuscript.

"You mean to put your name to the work?" he inquired.

"Yes, I do," answered William.

"Ah! Then I think we may venture on 500 copies, the publisher decided cautiously.

Great was the surprise when the entire stock was sold out within a few days of publication. Edition after edition was called for. In four months, 7,500 copies were circulated and still the demand continued.

The book became almost a "best-seller", and was translated into French, German, Italian, Spanish and Dutch.

The desire to write was not a sudden impulse. For years William had wanted, as he put it: "To address his countrymen on the important subject of religion." Some knew the secret of his life, but he wished to reach a larger circle. He wanted to "tell others"—to communicate the Gospel.

In the first chapter of his book William reminded his readers: "The Gospel is everywhere represented in Scripture by such figures as are most strongly calculated to impress on our minds a sense of its value. It is spoken of as light from darkness, as release from prison, as deliverance from captivity, as life from death."

In another chapter he describes what is meant by "believing in Jesus". He says it is no easy task.

"We must be deeply conscious of our guilt and misery, heartily repenting of our sins, and firmly

resolving to forsake them. We are to surrender our-
selves up to Him, to be 'washed in His blood', to
be sanctified by His Spirit, resolving to receive
Him for our Lord and Master, to learn in His
school and obey all His commandments."

As was usual in those days, William's work was
given a long title, fully describing its contents. It
became known for short as Wilberforce's *Practical
View*. It was aimed at the higher and middle classes
of society, and may be said to be a study of pre-
tended or superficial Christianity contrasted with
genuine or real Christianity.

Among the many thousands who read the book,
there were those who discovered in its pages the
remedy for their own deep spiritual need.

One of Scotland's greatest religious leaders,
Dr. Thomas Chalmers, acknowledged that the
book revolutionized his thinking, transformed his
life, and brought him into a genuine and personal
experience of Salvation.

\*  \*  \*

William's faith and courage led him into yet
further avenues of service.

Occasionally, he gave money to poor parsons in
country districts, for the purchase of Bibles. He
knew, however, that something on a much bigger
scale was necessary, in order to broadcast the
Word of God through the printed page. To his
delight, he soon found that others had been given
the vision also.

In December, 1802, the Rev. Thomas Charles

from Bala, North Wales, travelled to London to attend a Committee meeting of the Religious Tract Society (now known as the United Society for Christian Literature). The small company of solemn-faced, soberly dressed gentlemen was stirred to the depths, as Mr. Charles spoke. He told of the dire need of his people, for Bibles in the Welsh language.

He related the story of Mary Jones, the girl who walked twenty-five miles barefoot over the mountains to Bala to buy a Bible—and twenty-five miles back to her home. She had learned to read at the village school. For six years, she had been saving her pennies and half-pennies to purchase the precious book. She had done mending for neighbours, and looked after children; she had gathered sticks, and kept chickens—anything in fact, to earn a copper to put away in her money-box.

"Gentlemen," said Mr. Charles, "when she came to my house full of eagerness—even after such a journey—I had no Bible to give her."

The speaker paused, but the committee members were silent. He then continued: "When I told her there was a great shortage in the country, and I had not even one to spare, the poor child collapsed, and broke into uncontrollable weeping. I was upset and deeply moved. Seeing her distress, I felt I could not send her away without the book. What could I do? There were two or three copies locked away in my bookcase, reserved for earlier applicants. I took one of these from the shelf, and placed it in her hands.

"My child, this Bible is for you," I said.

She could scarcely believe it in view of my earlier remarks. In a little while, I was able to convince her, and her weeping was changed to unspeakable gratitude and joy.

"Gentlemen, we need Bibles," concluded the Rev. Thomas Charles. Having finished his appeal he sat down and waited. At length, the Rev. Joseph Hughes, the secretary, rose from his chair. "Surely a society might be formed for this purpose," he suggested, and then went on: "And if for Wales, why not for the kingdom, why not for the world?"

The Committee was impressed. From time to time, further discussions were held, and it was decided to invite the interest and support of Wilberforce and other members of the Clapham Sect.

On March 7, 1804, a new Society officially came into being—The British and Foreign Bible Society. William was elected a member of the first Committee, and became a very welcome speaker at the Annual Meetings. He regarded the circulation of the Scriptures throughout the world, as another important step in the cause of truth and freedom.

The spread of the Scriptures and missionary work go hand in hand. It was largely due to William's influence, and the exertions of the Rev. John Venn—the highly-esteemed pastor of the Clapham friends—that the Church Missionary Society was founded. It needed a lot of money to launch such worthy projects, and to keep them going. The members of the Clapham team were most generous in their giving to all evangelical work.

Before his marriage, William gave away at least one-quarter of his annual income. To the end of his life he was a strong believer in the Bible text: "God loveth a cheerful giver" (II Corinthians 9:7).

Yearly subscriptions were sent to almost every charitable institution in London, in Yorkshire, and as far away as Edinburgh. For financial help to promote her Sunday Schools, Hannah More could always count on William. When Charles Wesley died and his widow needed aid, William made her an annual allowance till her death in 1822. Indeed, not only prominent persons, but many a poor widow was helped because of his generosity. Young men in straitened circumstances, yet feeling the call to enter the Church, could look to him to assist with their college expenses. Peasant people with large families often had their burden made lighter by a gift from him.

William's love and sympathy flowed out to all in need. No doubt his own experience of ill-health and suffering created a bond of understanding. His general health was never really good, and he had the added disadvantage of being very short-sighted. Often he found reading and writing most difficult. As this disability was observed and regretted by his friends, it is perhaps not without significance that the Yorkshire School for the Blind was founded in 1833 to perpetuate his memory. The cost was met by public subscription. Situated in York, the school accepted blind children from the age of six, as well as the adult blind. Education was given, followed by training and useful employment.

The pioneers of this notable enterprise planned well, for the school continued through succeeding generations to the year 1968, when it was reconstituted as The Wilberforce Home for Multiple-Handicapped Blind. Not for Yorkshire alone, but for the whole of the United Kingdom, it provides a wonderful home for blind persons who have additional handicaps.

It is a splendid and fitting memorial to Wilberforce, known as the Member who served Yorkshire so well in Parliament, but best known as the man who freed the slaves.

# 11

## LOOKING AHEAD

BRITAIN was thoroughly war-weary, but it kept up the struggle against France. The Clapham team worked with abounding zeal through those years to spread the Gospel of Jesus Christ. India, as well as Africa, was dear to William's heart. Still, the master passion of his life remained the same—the abolition of slavery. He felt sure Parliament would be more ready to listen to his proposals, once the war was over. No one foresaw what a long-drawn-out conflict it would be. With short intermission it lasted for twenty-two years. Not until 1815 did the war finally end.

In spite of all the difficulties, things began to really move, however, in a practical way, when in 1807 the Bill for the Abolition of the Slave Trade became law.

The British Navy, the mistress of the seas, did a splendid job in sweeping the slave trade off the water, but it took time—many years in fact. William was often at the Admiralty asking for more anti-slavery patrols.

It was dangerous work. The British crews risked their lives along the mosquito-ridden slave coast of West Africa. The mangrove swamps were hotbeds of disease. Yellow fever, malaria and smallpox—those dreaded enemies of the white man—were common. Dysentery was rampant. Many sailors fell victims and died.

Yet the crews enjoyed the excitement of the chase, which could take twenty-four hours or more if the slaver was a fast-moving vessel. When captures were made, the crew could look forward to prize money from the Government, and the prospect of promotion. Many a captured slave-ship was burnt or smashed to pieces at Destruction Bay, Sierra Leone. Her slaves were freed and resettled at the Colony. All the principal countries of the western world had made the slave trade illegal by the year 1818—or had promised to do so. In practice, unfortunately, no serious efforts were made to enforce the law. Britain acted differently, for the Royal Navy made it virtually impossible for the slave trade to be carried on in British ships.

\*　　\*　　\*

As time went on William realized he must make some changes in his life, for in Parliament he had held the seat for Yorkshire for no less than thirty years. It was a strenuous and exacting task, and he saw little of his wife and family when Parliament was in session. Now his children had reached the age when they specially needed a father's guidance, so after much prayer and careful consideration, he resigned his seat in 1812, on the eve of another General Election. He did not, however, make a clear-cut retirement from the parliamentary scene. Instead, he accepted from Lord Calthorpe the pocket borough of Bramber—near the Sussex coast. Thus he was still in the House of Commons but with fewer responsibilities. He could be at home more often.

The next thing that William had to consider was the question of a successor who would lead the anti-slavery crusade when he himself could no longer do so. The goal was the abolition of slavery in British possessions. In view of the slow pace of parliamentary legislation, William felt that it was most unlikely that he would have the strength and vigour necessary for the final onslaught.

He reminded himself that in Old Testament times, Moses laid his hands upon Joshua in commission and blessing, and the younger man took over the leadership.

William looked around, and was drawn to a young man whom he heard speak at a meeting in the London Mansion House in 1816.

"That is the man for me," said William, as he listened to Thomas Fowell Buxton pleading on behalf of the poor in Spitalfields.

Two years later, Buxton entered Parliament as Member for Weymouth. He was a strong advocate for the reform of the Penal Code, and made a deep impression.

William was so passionately devoted to the Emancipation cause, that it was not easy for him to hand over the reins to another, yet he knew it was essential. In 1821, having had ample time to observe and appreciate Buxton's character and ability, Wilberforce took the decisive step. He wrote to Buxton, inviting him to lead "this holy enterprise", as he called the Abolition campaign.

Buxton accepted the new task. In the first years of partnership William continued in charge. Later, of course, Buxton took the full responsibility. It was soon evident to all that William had made a good choice, for Buxton was in complete sympathy with the Wilberforce crusade and greatly admired his chief. The newly appointed leader was in fact, no stranger to the problem of the African slaves. Born in 1786, he had heard of their plight from his earliest childhood, for his mother was a Quaker.

\* \* \*

"The time is ripe for another big battle," said the Abolitionists.

In the winter of 1822 they met in a "secret Cabinet Council", as William called it, to formulate their plans. Then William shut himself away from the world in his new country house at Marden Park, in order that he might concentrate on his latest Manifesto. This was published as a pamphlet of some fifty pages early in March, 1823. He had been urged by his friends to write his opinions "as to the state of the Negro slaves, the duty of improving it, and of gradually emancipating them". So effectively did he write that one West Indian planter who read the booklet, said to

William: "Your pamphlet has so affected me that, should it cost me my whole property, I surrender it willingly that my poor Negroes may be brought, not only to the liberty of Europeans but especially to the liberty of Christians."

This surprising tribute from an unexpected source pleased William greatly.

Then the Quakers drew up a Petition begging Parliament to redeem the hundreds of thousands of slaves in the British colonies. They asked William to present this to the House of Commons. In fulfilling this task William took the lead in Parliament for the last time. He presented the Petition on March 19, 1823, but it was Thomas Fowell Buxton who moved the Resolution on May 15, declaring that slavery was repugnant to Christianity and the British Constitution.

Buxton spoke boldly and did not evade the serious argument against emancipation which the opposition always put forward—the danger of a Negro insurrection.

"Wherever there is oppression there is danger," Buxton urged.

He went on: "The question is how that danger can be avoided. I assume it is to be avoided by giving liberty for slavery, happiness for misery."

A full debate followed. In the end, the head of Foreign Affairs, George Canning, won the day with his amendment. This advocated the policy of gradual improvement of the condition of the slaves, leading to full freedom later. Parliament approved the amendment. Once more the Government demonstrated that it was not yet ready to go all the way with the Abolitionists.

Though disappointed, both Wilberforce and Buxton were convinced that a sure foundation had been laid, and the day of the Negroes' liberation was a little nearer.

The planters were not alone in their fear of Negro revolt. William too, and some of his friends were also apprehensive—though for different reasons. They felt that the danger lay in the fact that the African slaves were kept in ignorance of the British Government's policy.

The planters hated any interference in their affairs, especially by the British Parliament. When therefore detailed instructions were received as to how the slaves were to be treated, the planters were angry. They did not like the new regulations forbidding the flogging of females, and the use of the whip in the field. Other measures of leniency towards the slaves were to follow, and some masters decided to keep the new rules hidden from the Negroes.

The result was that rumours began to circulate among the Negroes that the King of England had set them free, and their masters were unlawfully keeping them in bondage.

There was ferment everywhere. The most serious outburst was at Demerara, British Guiana. On the night of August 18, 1823, some 13,000 slaves rose and demanded immediate emancipation. They imprisoned the white men on their estates and ransacked their houses for arms, but they did not loot or burn down the buildings. In fact it was a most restrained uprising, but unfortunately two overseers were killed as they resisted the rebels.

The troops were called out and quickly put an end to the trouble. Only one soldier was wounded, but one hundred slaves were killed. The rest were savagely punished. There were many hangings and brutal floggings.

The disquieting news reached London in distorted and exaggerated form. Abuse was heaped upon Wilberforce and his friends. The newspapers blamed them for the insurrection. William was called a "vile hypocrite", and many other unpleasant names.

To the Christian public in Britain, a most distressing feature of the Demerara tragedy was the death sentence passed on the Rev. John Smith of the London Missionary Society. For seven years he had laboured to win the slaves for Christ, and they were devoted to him. When the insurrection broke out, John Smith, who was hated by the Governor and the planters, was arrested. He was accused of aiding and abetting the Negroes, and was tried by court-martial. The Colonial Fiscal conducted the prosecution. False witnesses were procured to give evidence against Smith, and he was compelled to testify against himself. Even in a slave-owning community the trial was a complete farce.

Smith did not go to the gallows, but died in

prison. His widow was not allowed to attend the funeral. When two Negro members of his congregation erected railings to mark his grave, the railings were torn down by his enemies.

The British Parliament took up the case, and William who was unwell, left his sick room to attend the debate. It taxed his strength considerably and sadly he realized that his days in Parliament were fast coming to an end.

Very reluctantly, Wilberforce retired in 1825 at the age of sixty-six. When for the last time he passed through the doors of the House of Commons, he carried history away with him. So much had happened since that day in 1780, when he had first entered the House. As he left, it gave him satisfaction to know that the Abolition cause would be maintained, for it had been committed to the safe hands of powerful advocates.

# 12

## ACHIEVEMENT

RETIRED! Yes, but not inactive. William was pleased that he could give more time to the Bible Society, and to his favourite missionary movements. He was still a frequent and welcome speaker at the Annual Meetings. His audiences were captivated by his radiant personality and his amazing eloquence. Robert Southey the poet, once said of William: "If ever there was a good and happy man on earth, he was one."

William himself was quick to attribute all his blessings to God, the source of every good and perfect gift. However, there was no doubt that he was able to communicate his faith and joy to others in a truly remarkable way.

To the end of his life his mind remained alert and clear. His friends never tired of listening to his reminiscences.

Wilberforce had seen Prime Ministers come and go, but in his opinion no one equalled William Pitt, and he often referred to their life-long friendship.

He was no stranger to Royalty; there had been a time when George III had asked him at the levée, "How go on your black clients, Mr. Wilberforce?"

In his later years William received one morning a message from the Duchess of Kent. He waited on her, and found her manner quite delightful, but it was her infant daughter who immediately attracted his attention. The bright little girl had her toys spread about the room. The elder statesman was soon down on the floor playing with the child who one day would become the great Queen Victoria.

Wilberforce lived through the long reign of George III; he saw George IV ascend to the Throne, and later the "sailor-king" William IV.

\*　　\*　　\*

Events were moving rapidly. May 14, 1833 was to be the first day of a decisive battle in Parliament, when once more the slavery question would be debated. The Abolitionists had been busy for some time. All over the country, meetings had been organized. Then delegates—three hundred strong —gathered in London and marched in a body to No. 10 Downing Street to present an Address to Earl Grey, the Prime Minister.

Petitions poured in from every quarter, the total number of signatures being almost a million and a half. It was a massive demonstration of public feeling in support of Negro emancipation.

William and his wife were at that time living in the home of their son Robert at East Farleigh, near Maidstone, Kent. Not content to merely put his signature to the Petition, William actually attended the Public Meeting in Maidstone, brushing aside doctor's orders, and the advice of his friends.

Despite his age and increasing frailty, Wilberforce addressed the meeting. Many a time his clear, ringing voice had filled the House of Commons; now the audience in the Town Hall had to listen very carefully to catch his words. One point he made absolutely clear—he believed that when the Negroes were freed, the slaveowners should be compensated for their loss.

"I say, and I say honestly and fearlessly, that the same Being Who commands us to love mercy, says also 'Do justice . . .' " he declared.

It was William's last public speech. A ray of sunlight streamed into the hall as gathering all his strength, he concluded triumphantly: "The object is bright before us; the light of heaven beams on it, and is an earnest of success."

Soon afterwards he was down with influenza.

Recovering a little, he went to Bath, but the famed waters of the Spa could not bring him back to health. On his return journey he stopped at the house of his cousin, Mrs. Lucy Smith. It was in Cadogan Place, within a mile of Westminster. The House of Commons sat debating the Abolition Bill put forward by the new Colonial Secretary, the Hon. Edward Geoffrey Stanley.

\*     \*     \*

The statesman saint lay dying. Swift messengers brought him news of the successive stages of the Bill.

On July 25, 1833, Parliament carried what has been described as "the noblest measure in its history". Quickly the tidings were despatched to Cadogan Place.

"Thank God I should have lived to witness a day in which England is willing to give twenty millions sterling for the Abolition of Slavery", William exclaimed.

The veteran crusader's work was done. Like the apostle Paul he had fought a good fight and finished his course. He died on July 29, 1833.

\* \* \*

London's crowds lined the city streets for the funeral. Public business was suspended and the shops were shut. Great numbers of people were in mourning. In the procession were the great men of the land—the bishops of the Church, the princes of the blood, and the King's chief servants. The pall-bearers were men of highest rank. At the Abbey the funeral procession was joined by Members of both Upper and Lower Houses of Parliament.

William Wilberforce was laid to rest in Westminster Abbey on August 5, 1833.

\* \* \*

A year later, the slaves were liberated. On the evening of July 31, the Negroes crowded into their churches. As the midnight hour drew near, they fell upon their knees in silent prayer. Not until the clocks struck twelve was that strange, breathless silence broken. Then as the ministers proclaimed: "The Negroes are free. The monster slavery is slain," the congregations leapt to their feet, and gave thanks to God for their deliverance.

Not in drunkenness and lawlessness, but quietly with a solemn, holy joy, they greeted the dawn.

The new day, August 1, 1834, heralded the fact that eight hundred thousand slaves had received their freedom.